WILLIAM LANGLAND

The probable author of *Piers Plowman*,
lived from *c.* 1332 to *c.* 1400.

WILLIAM LANGLAND

The Book Concerning
Piers the Plowman

RENDERED INTO
MODERN ENGLISH BY
DONALD AND RACHEL ATTWATER

EDITED BY
RACHEL ATTWATER, M.A.

DENT: LONDON
EVERYMAN'S LIBRARY
DUTTON: NEW YORK

NO. *571*

INTRODUCTION

THE POEM. The work called compendiously *The Book concerning Piers the Plowman* (*Liber de Petro Plowman*) is known in forty-seven manuscripts, in which scholars have agreed to recognize three versions of the text, called respectively the A-text, written soon after 1362; the B-text, written about 1378; and the C-text, written in 1398 or 1399. Each text contains two distinct parts (though they are not generally distinguished in the manuscripts), namely, The Vision of William concerning Piers the Plowman and the Vision of the same concerning Do-well, Do-better, and Do-best. The standard editions of these texts are those of Dr W. W. Skeat, published by the Early English Text Society, in four volumes, in 1867–84, and by the Clarendon Press in two volumes, 1886. The various known manuscripts are written in a mixture of the Midland and Southern dialects of Middle English, somewhat influenced by the Western dialect; but they vary considerably, both in dialect and text. That on which Professor Skeat based his B-text is MS. Laud Misc. 581 in the Bodleian Library.

THE AUTHOR. The authorship of this poem has been the subject of a wordy and involved dispute among literary historians and critics. The traditional view, resting partly on external but mainly on internal evidence, was that the author's christening name was William, for he refers to himself as Will in several passages, and his name is given as William in most of the manuscripts; that his surname was Langland (which is given in two early manuscripts, one of which adds the information that he was son of one Stacy de Rokayle, who held land at Shipton-under-Wychwood); that he was born at Cleobury Mortimer about 1332 (according to a writer one hundred and fifty years later); that he was put to school, probably with the Benedictines at Great Malvern; that he became a clerk in minor orders and wrote *The Book concerning Piers Plowman* (A-text) shortly after he had gone to London, where he later re-wrote and enlarged the poem (B-text); and he lived for many years on Cornhill with his wife Kit and his daughter Kalote (that he married accounts for his not being further ordained); that he earned a precarious and poor living by such clerical means (in both senses) as he might, that he wore the clerical tonsure and dress, and that he was so tall as to be known familiarly as Long Will; that he again revised his poem (C-text), and died we know not when nor where.

With minor variations this account of the writer and the writing of the poem was accepted without question until the beginning of this century, when Professor J. M. Manly produced a theory, supported by textual evidence, that the poem was written not by one but by five persons: not, of course, in concert, but as independent editors and continuers. This provoked a very pretty battle of the kind in which literary historians and textual critics delight. Dr Furnivall and Dr Henry Bradley, with some hesitation, supported the conclusions of Professor Manly; and M. Jusserand led the single-author party, whose case was strengthened by the researches of Professor R. W. Chambers: articles, replies, pamphlets, rejoinders, letters and counter-letters were written and published; Langland was 'on trial for his life,' he was sentenced, hanged, drawn, quartered, and resuscitated— several times over.

But in spite of the difficulties raised by these learned men, it may be said with confidence that the balance of literary, textual, philological, and metrical evidence is still on the side of a single author; and that this author was William Langland has found fresh and valuable support in later investigations of a kind too little used in the solving of literary and historical puzzles, namely, research, inquiry, and observation in the neighbourhood concerned. It appears clear from the work of Mr Allan H. Bright (*New Light on 'Piers Plowman,'* Oxford, 1928) that we may continue to hold undisturbed the traditional account of Long Will, with two important modifications, namely, that he was born not at Cleobury in Cheshire but at Ledbury in Hereford-shire, and that he was the *illegitimate* son of Stacy de Rokayle.

THIS VERSION. Of the prologue and first seven *passus* of the B-text, for the version of which herein I alone am responsible, several translations into modern English have been made. My object in making another was simply and solely to produce a version with the minimum of alteration and verbal substitution of the Middle English text necessary for its understanding by an ordinary reader in the twentieth century. To do this, and at the same time always to retain the original alliterative metre, was impossible; nor did this grieve me overmuch: for Langland himself kept on breaking the metrical rules, either because he was more interested in the sense than the sound, or else because he did not think regularity necessary to make a good poem—he was no 'literary man,' and his academic fame to-day doubtless astonishes him. I paraphrased as little as possible, preferring a few obscurities to excessive messing about with the text. Those who wish for a straightforward version, in prose and with all things made clear, cannot do better than that of Miss Kate Warren (London, 1913); for a metrical version, with the poem sacrificed to the verse, there is that of Professor Skeat (London, 1905): I used both of these for reference purposes, especially Miss Warren's, which is an excellent piece of work.

Without the erudition and monumental labours of Professor Skeat this version would have been impossible, and I have to make acknowledgment to the Delegates of the Oxford University Press for their permission to use his B-text, the minor edition in the Clarendon Press Series, of which the ninth edition was published in 1906. I must also acknowledge my indebtedness for help and information to Mr Allan H. Bright.

THE THEME. Whatever may be the literary, philological, and historical importance of *The Book concerning Piers Plowman*, its interest to the ordinary reader is still the same as it was to its writer, namely, personal. I have said that Langland was not a 'literary man,' least of all in the self-conscious modern sense— perhaps the expression has no other sense: anyway, he was not primarily a man of art but a man of prudence, in fact, a moralist. And his poem is a tract. Therein is its interest to-day as in the fourteenth century; that is why it is republished in cheap editions and read by others beside professors and students. However much human nature may change superficially, men continue to have a bias towards inordinate behaviour in thought, word, and deed, and so long as we have that characteristic, whether the resulting disorder be regarded as 'sinful' or as simply 'anti-social,' so long will moralists, professional or amateur, rise up and endeavour to reduce us to the ways of virtue.

And the miserable sinners, however unwilling we may be to be cured of our distemper, are far from being uninterested in the attempts to do so; some even acquire considerable skill in criticism of the efforts; and this interest in our physicians is not an exhibition of diabolical cynicism. For we know that the moralist is really in the right of it; that the heart of man does tend to be desperately wicked—however you like to account for it; that left to ourselves we shall make a hell of this world and deserve the same in the next; that God is not mocked.

So Langland's poem is read, not indeed deliberately as an ascetical exercise, but because it is a good tract, a bit of moralist's work well done: the poem and the argument are one thing, and that thing gratifies our mind in general and satisfies our conscience in particular.

Those who have never read the book commonly suppose it to be an attack on the iniquities of those in places of power and advantage, especially of spiritual authority: that the author was a morning-star of the Reformation and a forerunner of what is called modern democracy. This is a complete misunderstanding. Langland was a faithful son of the medieval Church, and his politics were anything but 'radical': the State should be governed by a Prince, the personification but not the nominee or the tool of his people, whom he rules with the aid of Conscience and Reason. And his attack on wickedness and abuses was not by way of direct denouncement, of rhetoric (in its improper sense), or a playing on the feelings of a mob; but a logical explanation directed at common sense and right reason. 'This,' he said in effect, 'is how you behave, poor and rich, lowly as well as great. Of course it must follow that the world is in a mess and you are unhappy.' There is none of the demagoguery which flatters our self-esteem and tickles our lust for change, telling us what fine fellows we are and that it is our institutions that are at fault. On the contrary. He makes it clear enough to his contemporaries that their institutions were all right, but their human weakness and ill-will misused them or made them helpless. 'Christianity has been tried and has failed.' 'It has not failed because it has not been tried.' Langland's one remedy for the troubles of his day was religion: he was therefore not a social reformer in the classical sense.

The efforts of moralists, especially Christian moralists, are less effective than they should be, and bring down dislike and contempt on their makers, because the impression is so often given that the moralist views with jealousy, or is trying improperly to narrow the bounds of, lawful human enjoyment. The notion is quite wrong and quite understandable. The average professional moralist has only average insight, energy, enthusiasm, and spirituality; and so he takes the easiest line, concentrates on the more obviously disorderly actions and abuses of acts intrinsically good, and denounces and exhorts with a lamentable lack of discrimination and finesse, meeting exaggeration with exaggeration.

Not so Langland. 'Chastity without charity shall be chained in Hell,' he says, and has done. Charity, that is, not a vague benevolence, a 'universal embrace,' or even just refraining from adverse speech and being kind (especially to those one likes), but the habit or virtue which enables men to love God above all things for His own sake and for His sake to love all their fellow men; the *agape* of St Paul. It goes to the root of the matter, psychologically, theologically, and spiritually. He does not exhort his hearers to fantastic penances, to heroic renunciations, to revolutionary changes, to action against their proper state and personal nature: the rich are not abused for being rich, but told to have pity on the poor; the poor are to work and not over-reach their neighbours; the monk is not told to leave his cloister and get busy in the world, for prayer is work, and Christ ordained the contemplative life; those who will not work shall be coerced by Hunger, yet no beggar must be refused *quia incertum pro quo Deo magis placeas*; trade is not condemned, but merchants must try to be honest (Langland does not seem very hopeful about this); neither is the law condemned, but lawyers must observe equity; nothing shall be done out of measure. In a word, he preaches on the text of St Augustine: *Dilige et quod vis fac*, Love, and do what you will.

Joined with Charity as handmaidens of Truth (God the Father) is Reason. Charity is not personified in the poem, but Reason is, and the part he plays may be studied profitably both by those who have old-fashioned ideas about the 'ages of faith' and those who have new-fashioned and sub-human ideas about the worthlessness of intellectual processes. To Reason Conscience appeals against his projected wedding to Meed ('Graft'); with Conscience he is made the perpetual counsellor of the King; and his sermon moves the Deadly Sins to confess themselves to Repentance. Then, and not till then, towards the end of Passus V, does Piers himself appear on the scene, and he quickly develops from the hard-working, God-fearing yeoman farmer, taught by Truth through Conscience and Mother-Wit, into what is practically an incarnation of God the Son, embodying in himself Reason, Conscience, Mother-Wit, and the rest. Christ, as man, is the common man, Piers Plowman. To him God the Father entrusts the dispensing of a bull of pardon surpassing all others, that supreme indulgence which is man's Redemption and the price of which is good deeds, both spiritual and corporal.

DONALD ATTWATER.

1930.

The second part of the poem, *The Vision of Do-well, Do-better, and Do-best*, is a broadening and deepening of the theme. The strictures on the life of the world, and especially on the ways of church dignitaries in relation to that world, are still there in abundance. But Langland is primarily examining the fundamental principles on which his strictures rest. What is in fact 'the good life'? What is it to do well, to do better, and to do best? His illustrations and parallels are many and varied, but they are finally all taken up into the life of our Lord, and especially His death and resurrection. The poem, however, does not end on any such devotional climax. In Passus XIX Langland returns, or rather goes forward, to the church of to-day, as it were, working, suffering, fighting the arrayed forces of evil and betrayals from within not always with conspicuous success. Finally Conscience, in great distress, sets out to seek Piers the Plowman—Langland's continued symbol of integrity, from the man working in the field to Christ Himself. The pilgrimage has only just begun.

In making a version of the B-text of *The Vision of Do-well, Do-better, and Do-best* I have followed the same principles as those which directed the version of *The Vision of Piers Plowman*; that is, making changes only as it was necessary for clarification for the modern reader. It has been attempted to preserve the style of Langland, his own peculiar 'flavour,' which includes not only variety but a lack of academic care (if we do not call it carelessness) which makes such treatment not only possible but rewarding.

RACHEL ATTWATER.

1957.

SELECT BIBLIOGRAPHY

EDITIONS. W. W. Skeat: *The Vision of William concerning Piers the Plowman.* 2 vols. Oxford, 1886 (the standard edition of all three texts); *Publications of the Early English Text Society,* Nos. 28, 38, 54, 81 (separate editions of A, B, and C Texts, with notes and glosses).

TRANSLATIONS. W. W. Skeat: *The Vision of Piers Plowman,* London (1906); K. M. Warren: *The Vision of Piers the Plowman,* London (1913) (Prose. Prologue and Passus, B Text); H. W. Wells: *The Vision of Piers Plowman,* London (1935) (Verse. Whole poem); N. K. Coghill: *Visions from Piers Plowman,* London (1949) (Verse. Selections); J. F. Goodridge: *Piers the Ploughman,* Harmondsworth (1959) (Prose. Complete poem, B Text).

STUDIES. (*a*) *General*

D. Chadwick: *Social Life in the Days of Piers Plowman,* Cambridge (1922); R. W. Chambers: 'Long Will, Dante, and the Righteous Heathen,' *Essays and Studies,* 9; N. K. Coghill: 'The Character of Piers Plowman considered from the B Text,' in *Medium Aevum,* 2. 108–135, 1933; F. A. R. Carnegy: *The Relations between the Social and Divine Order in William Langland's Vision,* Breslau (1934); G. Hort: *Piers Plowman and Contemporary Religious Thought,* London (1938); R. W. Chambers: *Man's Unconquerable Mind,* chs. 4 and 5, London (1939); N. K. Coghill: *The Pardon of Piers Plowman,* London (1946).

(*b*) *Authorship, date, construction*

The Piers Plowman Controversy. Publications of the Early English Text Society, 139. Extra issue, 1910 (essays by Jusserand, Manly, Chambers, and Bradley); R. W. Chambers: 'Text of Piers Plowman: Critical Methods,' in *Modern Language Review* (Cambridge), *11.* 257–275 (1916); 'The Three Texts of Piers Plowman and their Grammatical Forms,' in *Modern Language Review,* *14.* 129–51 (1919); 'The Text of Piers Plowman' (with Grattan) in *Modern Language Review,* *26.* 1–51 (1926); A. H. Bright: *New Light on 'Piers Plowman,'* London (1928); J. A. W. Bennett: 'The Date of the B Text of Piers Plowman' in *Medium Aevum,* 11. 55–64 (1943); G. H. Gerould: 'The Structural Integrity of Piers Plowman' in *Studies in English Philology,* *45.* 60–75 (1948); J. R. Hulbert: 'Piers the Plowman after Forty Years' in *Modern Philology* (Chicago), *45.* 215–25 (1948); B. F. Huppé: 'Piers Plowman: the Date of the B Text Reconsidered' in *Studies in English Philology,* *46.* 6–13 (1949).

PUBLISHER'S NOTE

The Donald Attwater translation of *The Vision* is reproduced here by arrangement with Messrs Cassell & Co. Ltd.   *Do-well, Do-better and Do-best* is based on Dr Skeat's edition (1886) by permission of the Clarendon Press, Oxford.

CONTENTS

The poem is written in the traditional long alliterative line which is divided in two by a caesura, each part being linked by alliteration or 'initial rhyme.' In the present rendering this pause is indicated by a space.

INCIPIT LIBER
DE PETRO PLOWMAN

PROLOGUS

In a summer season   when soft was the sun,
I clothed myself in a cloak   as I shepherd were,
Habit like a hermit's   unholy in works,
And went wide in the world   wonders to hear.
But on a May morning   on Malvern hills,
A marvel befell me   of fairy, methought.
I was weary with wandering   and went me to rest
Under a broad bank   by a brook's side,
And as I lay and leaned over   and looked into the waters
I fell into a sleep   for it sounded so merry.

Then began I to dream   a marvellous dream,
That I was in a wilderness   wist I not where.
As I looked to the east   right into the sun,
I saw a tower on a toft   worthily built;
A deep dale beneath   a dungeon therein,
With deep ditches and dark   and dreadful of sight.
A fair field full of folk   found I in between,
Of all manner of men   the rich and the poor,
Working and wandering   as the world asketh.
Some put them to plow   and played little enough,
At setting and sowing   they sweated right hard
And won that which wasters   by gluttony destroy.

Some put them to pride   and apparelled themselves so
In a display of clothing   they came disguised.

To prayer and penance   put themselves many,
All for love of our Lord   living hard lives,
In hope for to have   heavenly bliss.
Such as anchorites and hermits   that kept them in their cells,
And desired not the country   around to roam;
Nor with luxurious living   their body to please.

And some chose trade   they fared the better,
As it seemeth to our sight   that such men thrive.

B 57I   1

And some to make mirth   as minstrels know how,
And get gold with their glees   guiltlessly, I hold.
But jesters and janglers   children of Judas,
Feigning their fancies   and making folk fools,
They have wit at will   to work, if they would;
Paul preacheth of them   I'll not prove it here—
Qui turpiloquium loquitur   is Lucifer's hind.

    Tramps and beggars   went quickly about,
Their bellies and their bags   with bread well crammed:
Cadging for their food   fighting at ale;
In gluttony, God knows   going to bed,
And getting up with ribaldry   the thieving knaves!
Sleep and sorry sloth   ever pursue them.

    Pilgrims and palmers   pledged them together
To seek Saint James   and saints in Rome.
They went forth on their way   with many wise tales,
And had leave to lie   all their life after—
I saw some that said   they had sought saints:
Yet in each tale that they told   their tongue turned to lies
More than to tell truth   it seemed by their speech.

    Hermits, a heap of them   with hooked staves,
Were going to Walsingham   and their wenches too;
Big loafers and tall   that loth were to work,
Dressed up in capes   to be known from others;
And so clad as hermits   their ease to have.

    I found there friars [1]   of all the four orders,
Preaching to the people   for profit to themselves,
Explaining the Gospel   just as they liked,
To get clothes for themselves   they construed it as they would.
Many of these master friars   may dress as they will,
For money and their preaching   both go together.
For since charity hath been chapman   and chief to shrive lords,
Many miracles have happened   within a few years.
Except Holy Church and they   agree better together,
Great mischief on earth   is mounting up fast.

    There preached a pardoner [2]   as if he priest were:
He brought forth a brief   with bishops' seals thereon,
And said that himself might   absolve them all
From falseness in fasting   and of broken vows.

    Laymen believed him   welcomed his words,

[1] See page 202.   [2] See page 202.

And came up on their knees   to kiss his seals;
He cozened them with his brevet   dimmed their eyes,
And with his parchment   got his rings and brooches:
Thus they gave their gold   gluttons to keep.
And lend it to such louts   as follow lechery.
If the bishop were holy   and worth both his ears,
His seal should not be sent   to deceive the people.
But a word 'gainst bishop   the knave never preacheth.
Parish priest and pardoner   share all the silver
That the parish poor would have   if he were not there.
   Parsons and parish priests   complained to the bishop
That their parishes were poor   since the pestilence time,
And asked leave and licence   in London to dwell
And sing *requiems* for stipends   for silver is sweet.
   Bishops and bachelors [1]   both masters and doctors,
That have charge under Christ   and the tonsure as token
And sign that they should   shrive their parishioners,
Preach and pray for them   and feed the poor,
These lodge in London in Lent   and at other times too.
Some serve the king   and his silver count
In Chequer and Chancery courts   making claim for his debts
Of wards and of wardmotes   waifs and estrays.
And some serve as servants   to lords and ladies,
And instead of stewards   sit in session to judge.
Their Mass and their matins   their canonical hours,
Are said undevoutly   I fear at the last
Lest Christ in his council   accurse will full many.
I perceived of the power   that Peter had to keep,
To bind and to unbind   as the Book telleth,
How he left it with love   as our Lord ordained,
Amongst four virtues   the best of all virtues,
That cardinal are called   for they hinge the gates
Where Christ is in glory   to close and to shut
And to open it to them   and show heavenly bliss.
But of cardinals at Rome   that received that name
And power presumed in them   a pope to make,
To have Peter's power   deny it I will not;
For to love and learning   that election belongeth,
Therefore I can, and yet cannot   of that court speak more.
   Then came there a king   with knighthood before him,

[1] See page 202.

The might of the commons   made him to reign;
Then came Mother-Wit   and he made wise clerks
For to counsel the king   and the commons save.
    The king and the knighthood   the clergy as well,
Planned that the commons   should provide for themselves.
    The commons contrived   of Mother-Wit, crafts,
And for profit of all   they plowmen ordained
To till and travail   as true life asketh.
The king and the commons   and Mother-Wit too
Cause by law and loyalty   each man to know his own.
    Then looked up a lunatic   a lean thing withal,
And kneeling before the king   well speaking said:
'Christ keep thee sir King   and thy kingdom,
And grant thee to rule the realm   so Loyalty may love thee,
And for thy rightful ruling   be rewarded in heaven.'
    Then in the air on high   an angel of heaven
Stooped and spoke in Latin   for simple men could not
Discuss nor judge   that which should justify them,
But should suffer and serve   therefore said the angel:

    'Sum Rex, sum Princeps: neutram fortasse deinceps;
      O qui jura regis Christi specialia regis, hoc quod agas melius justus es,
        esto pius!
      Nudum jus a te vestiri vult pietate; qualia vis metere talia grana sere.
      Si jus nudatur nudo de jure metatur; si seritur pietas de pietate metas.'

    Then an angry buffoon   a glutton of words,
To the angel on high   answered after:

    'Dum rex a regere dicatur nomen habere,
      Nomen habet sine re nisi studet jura tenere.'

    Then began all the commons   to cry out in Latin,
For counsel of the king   construe how-so he would:

    'Praecepta regis sunt nobis vincula legis.'

[1] With that there ran a rout   of rats at once,
And small mice with them   more than a thousand,
And came to a council   for their common profit;
For a cat from the Court   came when he liked
And o'er leaped them lightly   and caught them at will,
Played with them perilously   and pushed them about.
'For dread of divers dangers   we dare not look about;
If we grumble at his game   he will attack us all,
Scratch us or clutch us   and in his claws hold us,

                  [1] See page 202.

So that we loathe life   ere he lets us go.
Could we with any wit   his will withstand
We might be lords above him   and live at our ease.'
   A rat of renown   most ready of tongue
Said, as a sovereign   help to himself:
'I have seen men,' quoth he   'in the city of London
Bearing bright necklaces   about their necks,
Some with collars of skilful work   uncoupled they wander
Both in warrens and wastes   wherever they like;
And otherwhile they are elsewhere   as I tell you.
Were there a bell on their collars   by Jesus, I think
Men might know where they went   and get out of their way!
And right so,' quoth that rat   'reason me showeth
To buy a brass bell   or one of bright silver
Make it fast to a collar   for our common profit,
And hang it on the cat's neck   then we may hear
When he romps or rests   or runneth to play.
And if he wants play   then we may look out
And appear in his presence   the while he play liketh,
And if he gets angry, beware   and shun all his paths.'
All this rout of rats   to this plan assented.
But though the bell was bought   and on the collar hanged,
There was not a rat in the rout   for all the realm of France
That dare bind on the bell   about the cat's neck,
Nor hang it round her ears   all England to win;
They held themselves not bold   and their counsel feeble,
Esteemed their labour as lost   and all their long plotting.
   A mouse that knew much more   as it seemed to me,
Ran forth determined   and stood before them all,
And to the rout of rats   rehearsed these words:
'Though we killed the cat   yet there would come another,
To scratch us and all our kind   though we creep under benches.
Therefore I counsel all the commons   to let the cat be,
And be we never so bold   to show to him the bell;
For I heard my sire say   now seven years ago,
"When the cat is a kitten   the Court is right wretched,"
As witnesseth Holy Writ   whoso will it read:
     "*Vae tibi, terra, cujus rex puer est.*"
No man can have rest there   for the rats by night;
While the cat catcheth conies   he covets not our carrion,
But feeds himself on venison   may we never defame him!

For better is a little loss   than a long sorrow;
He's the fear among us all   whereby we miss worse things.
For many men's malt   we mice would destroy,
And the riot of rats   would rend men's clothes,
Were it not for that Court cat   that can leap in among you;
For had ye rats your will   ye could not rule yourselves.
As for me,' quoth the mouse   'I see so much to come
That cat nor kitten never shall   by my counsel be harmed,
Nor carping of this collar   that cost me nothing.
Though it had cost me full dear   I would not own to it
But suffer him to live   and do just as he liketh:
Coupled and uncoupled   to catch what they can.
Therefore each wise wight I warn   to watch well his own.'
    What this dream meaneth   ye men that be merry,
Divine ye, for I never dare   by dear God in heaven!
    There hovered an hundred   in caps of silk,
Serjeants they seemed   who practised at Bar,
Pleading the law   for pennies and pounds,
And never for love of our Lord   unloosing their lips.
You might better measure the mist   on the Malvern hills,
Than get a sound out of their mouth   unless money were showed.
    Barons and burgesses   and bondmen also
I saw in this crowd   as you shall hear later.
Bakers and brewers   and butchers a-many,
Woollen-websters   and weavers of linen,
Tailors and tinkers   toll-takers in markets,
Masons and miners   and men of all crafts.
Of all kinds of labourers   there stood forth some;
Ditchers and diggers   that do their work ill
And spend all the day singing   '*Dieu vous sauve, dame Emme!*'
Cooks and their knaves   cried 'Pies, hot pies!
Good pork and good goose!   Come, dine! Come, dine!'
    Taverners unto them   told the same tale:
'White wine of Alsace   red wine of Gascony,
Wine of the Rhine, of Rochelle   to help settle your meat!'
All this I saw sleeping   and seven times more.

PASSUS I

What this mountain meaneth   and the dark dale
And the field full of folk   I fairly will show.
A lady, lovely of looks   in linen clothed,
Came down from a castle   and called me fairly
And said: 'Son, sleepest thou?   Seest thou this people,
How busy they be   about all the throng?
The most part of this people   that passeth on earth,
Have worship in this world   and wish for no better;
Of other heaven than here   they hold no account.'
  I was feared of her face   though she were so fair,
And said, 'Mercy, madam   what is this to mean?'
'The tower on the toft,' quoth she   'Truth is therein
And would have that ye do   as his word teacheth;
For he is Father of Faith   formed you all
Both with flesh and with face   and gave you fine wits
To worship him therewith   while that ye are here.
Therefore he hath bade the earth   to help you each one
With woollen, with linen   with food at your need,
In reasonable measure   to make you at ease.
  'And commanded of his courtesy   three things in common.
None are needful but those   and name them I will
And reckon them rightly   rehearse thou them after.
The first one is vesture   to save thee from chill;
And meat for meals   to save thee misease
And drink when thou art dry   but do naught out of reason
Lest thy worth be wanting   when thou shouldest work.
  'For Lot in his lifetime   for liking of drink
Did with his daughters   what the Devil liked.
He delighted in drink   as the Devil wished,
And Lechery was gainer   and lay with them both,
Putting blame on the wine   for that wicked deed:
  Inebriamus eum vino, dormiamusque cum eo, ut servare possimus de
      patre nostro semen.
Through wine and through women   there was Lot overcome,
Begetting in gluttony   boys that were blackguards.

7

Therefore dread delicious drink   and thou shalt do the better;
Measure is medicine   though thou yearn for much.
All is not good for the spirit   that the guts asketh,
Nor livelihood to thy body   that is life to the soul.
Believe not thy body   for him a liar teacheth:
That is, the wretched world   which would thee betray.
For the fiend and thy flesh   follow thee together;
This and that chaseth thy soul   and speak in thine heart;
That thou shouldest be ware   I teach thee the best.'
    'Madam, mercy,' quoth I   'I like well your words.
But the money of this earth   that men hold to so fast,
Tell me, madam, to whom   that treasure belongeth?'
    'Go to the Gospel,' quoth she   'that God spoke himself,
When the people posed him   with a penny in the Temple,
Whether they should therewith   worship king Caesar.
And God asked of them   of whom spake the writing
And likewise the image   that stood thereon?
"*Caesaris*," they said   "Each one sees him well."
    '"*Reddite Caesari*," quoth God   "that *Caesari* belongeth,
Et quae sunt Dei, Deo   or else ye do ill."
For rightful Reason   should rule you all,
And Mother-Wit be warden   your wealth to keep,
And tutor of your treasure   to give it you at need;
For husbandry and they   hold well together.'
Then I asked her plainly   by him that made her,
'That dungeon in the dale   that dreadful is to see,
What may it mean   *ma dame*, I beseech you?'
    'That is the castle of Care   whoso cometh therein
May curse he was born   in body or in soul.
Therein abideth a wight   that is called Wrong,
Father of Falsehood   who built it himself.
Adam and Eve   he egged on to ill;
Counselled Cain   to kill his brother;
Judas he jockeyed   with Jewish silver,
And then on an elder   hanged him after.
He is the letter of love   and lieth to all;
Those who trust in his treasure   betrayeth he soonest.'
    Then had I wonder in my wit   what woman it were
That such wise words   of Holy Writ showed,
And asked her in the high name   ere she thence went,
Who indeed she was   that taught me so fairly?

'Holy Church I am,' quoth she　'thou oughtest me to know.
I received thee first　and taught thee the faith,
And thou broughtest me sponsors　my bidding to fulfil
And to love me loyally　while thy life lasteth.'
　Then I fell on my knees　and cried of her grace,
And prayed her piteously　to pray for my sins,
And to teach me kindly　on Christ to believe,
That I might work his will　that made of me man.
'Show me no treasure　but tell me this only—
How may I save my soul　thou that holy art held?'
　'When all treasures are tried,' quoth she　'truth is the best;
I appeal to *Deus caritas*　to tell thee truth;
It is as dear a darling　as dear God himself.
　'Whoso is true of his tongue　and telleth none other,
And doth works therewith　and willeth no man ill:
He is a god, says the Gospel　on earth and in heaven,
And like to our Lord　by Saint Luke's own words.
The clergy that know this　should tell it about,
For Christian and heathen　alike claim the truth.
　'Kings and their knights all　should care for it rightly;
Ride to reach the oppressors　all round the realms,
And take *trangressores*　tying them tightly,
Till Truth had determined　the tale of their trespass.
That profession plainly　pertaineth to knights;
Not to fast on one Friday　in five score winters,
But hold with him and with her　that desireth all truth
And never leave them for love　nor for seizing of silver.
　'For David in his days　dubbed knights,
And swore them on their swords　to serve Truth ever;
And whoso passed that point　*apostata* was from the order.
　'But Christ, king of all kings　ten orders knighted,
Cherubim and Seraphim　seven such and one other,
And gave them might of his majesty　the merrier they thought it;
And over his common court　made them archangels,
Taught them by the Trinity　the truth to know
And to bow to his bidding　he bade them naught else.
　'Lucifer with his legions　learned it in Heaven,
But because he obeyed not　his bliss he did lose,
And fell from that fellowship　in a fiend's likeness
Into a deep dark hell　to dwell there for ever;
And more thousands with him　than man could number

Leapt out with Lucifer   in loathly form:
For they believed in him   that lied in this manner—
    Ponam pedem in aquilone, et similis ero altissimo.
    'And all that hoped it might be so   no Heaven might hold them;
They fell out in fiend's likeness   nine days together,
Till God of his goodness   steadied and stayed
Made the heavens to be shut   and stand so in quiet.
    'When these wicked went out   wonderwise they fell;
Some in air, some in earth   and some in deep hell;
But Lucifer lowest   lieth of them all.
For the pride he put on   his pain hath no end;
And all that work wrong   wander they shall
After their death day   and dwell with that wretch.
But those that work well   as holy writ telleth,
And end, as I have said   in truth, that is best,
May be sure that their soul   shall wend to Heaven,
Where Truth is in Trinity   and enthroneth them all.
Therefore I say, as I said   in sight of these texts,
When all treasures are tried   Truth is the best.
Learn these unlearned   for lettered men know it,
That Truth is treasure   the best tried on earth.'
    'Yet have I no natural knowing,'[1] quoth I   'ye must teach me better,
By what craft of my body   begins it, and where.'
    'Thou doting duffer,' quoth she   'dull are thy wits;
Too little Latin thou learnest   man, in thy youth;
    Heu mihi, quod sterilem duxi vitam juvenilem!
    'It is natural knowing,' quoth she   'that teacheth thine heart
For to love thy good Lord   liefer than thyself;
No deadly sin to do   die though thou shouldest:
This I trow to be Truth   who can teach thee better,
See you suffer him to say   and then teach it after.
For thus witnesseth his words   work thou thereafter;
For Truth telleth that Love   is the remedy of Heaven;
No sin may be seen in him   that useth that sort,
And all his works he wrought   with Love as he listed;
And taught it Moses for the best thing   and most like to Heaven
With the plant of peace   most precious of virtues.
    'For Heaven might not hold it   so heavy of itself,
Till it had of the earth   eaten its fill.
    'And when it had of this fold   flesh and blood taken,

[1] See page 202.

Never was leaf upon linden   lighter thereafter,
And pricking and piercing   as the point of a needle,
That no armour might stay it   nor any high walls.
  'Therefore is Love leader   of the Lord's folk of Heaven,
And a mean, as the mayor is   between king and commons;
Right so is Love a leader   and the law shapeth,
Upon man for his misdeeds   he fixeth the fine.
And for to know it by nature   it springeth in might,
In the heart is its head   and there its well-spring.
  'For in natural knowing   there might beginneth
That comes from the Father   that formed us all,
Looked on us with love   and let his Son die
Meekly for our misdeeds   to amend us all;
And yet would he them no woe   that wrought him that pain,
But meekly with his mouth   mercy he besought
To have pity of that people   that pained him to death.
  'Here might thou see examples   in himself alone,
That he was mightful and meek   and mercy did grant
To them that hanged him on high   and pierced his heart.
  'Therefore I rede you rich   to have pity on the poor;
Though ye be mighty at law   be meek in your works.
  'For the same measures that ye mete   amiss or aright,
Ye shall be weighed therewith   when ye wend hence;
     Eadem mensura qua mensi fueritis, remetietur vobis.
  'For though ye be true of your tongue   and honestly earn,
And as chaste as a child   that weepeth in church,
Unless ye love loyally   and give to the poor,
Such goods as God sends you   to them gladly giving,
Ye have no more merit   in Mass or in hours
Than Malkin of her maidenhood   that no man desireth.
  'For James the gentle   judged in his books
That faith without deed   is right nothing worth
And as dead as a door-post   unless actions follow;
     Fides sine operibus mortua est, etc.
  'Therefore chastity without charity   shall be chained in hell;
It is lacking as a lamp   that no light is in.
Many churchmen are chaste   but their charity is away;
Are no men more avaricious   when they be advanced:
Unkind to their kin   and to all Christian folk,
They chew up their charity   and chide after more.
Such chastity without charity   shall be chained in hell.

'Many pastors keep themselves   clean in their bodies
But are cumbered with covetousness   they can not drive it from them
So hardly hath avarice   hasped them together.
And that is no truth of the Trinity   but treachery of hell,
Lessoning the unlearned   to withhold their alms.
    'Therefore these words   are written in the Gospel,
Date et dabitur vobis   for I give to you all.
And that is the lock of Love   that letteth out my grace
To comfort the care-full   encumbered with sin.
    'Love is leech of life   and next our Lord's self,
And also the right road   that runneth unto Heaven;
Therefore I say as I said   before by the texts,
When all treasures be tried   Truth is the best.
Now have I told thee what Truth is   that no treasure is better;
I may linger no longer thee with   now look on thee our Lord!'

Yᴇᴛ I knelt on my knees   and cried of her grace,
And said: 'Mercy, Madame   for Mary's love of Heaven.
That bore that blissful Child   that bought us on the rood,
Teach me by some skilled way   Falsehood to know.'
    'Look upon thy left side   and lo! where he standeth,
Both Falsehood and Flattery   and their many fellows!'
    I looked on my left side   as the lady taught me,
And was ware of a woman   worthily clothed,
With fringes of fur   the finest on earth,
Crowned with a crown   the king hath no better
Featly her fingers   were framed with gold wire,
And thereon red rubies   as red as any coal,
And diamonds of dearest price   and two kinds of sapphires,
Orientals and beryls   poison banes to destroy.
    Her robe was full rich   of red scarlet dyed,
With ribands of red gold   and of richest stones;
Her array me ravished   such riches saw I never;
I had wonder what she was   and whose wife she were.
    'What is this woman,' quoth I   'so worthily attired?'
'That is Meed[1] the Maid,' quoth she   'who hath vexed me full oft,
And lied of my lover   that Loyalty is called,
And slandered him to lords   that have to guard laws;
In the pope's palace   familiar as myself,
Though truth would not so   for she is a bastard.
    'For Flattery was her father   that had a fickle tongue
And never said sooth   since he came to earth.
And Meed is mannered after him   right as nature requireth;
        Qualis pater, talis filius bona arbor bonum fructum facit.
    'I ought to be higher than she   my birth is the better.
My father the great God is   and ground of all graces,
One infinite God   and I his good daughter;
And he gave me Mercy   to marry with myself.
And what man be merciful   and loyally me love
Shall be my lord, I his lover   in highest Heaven.
    'And what man taketh Meed   mine head dare I lay
That he shall lose for her love   a lot of *caritatis*.
How construeth David the king   of men that take Meed

[1] See page 202.

13

And of men of this mould   that maintaineth Truth
And how ye shall save yourselves   the Psalter beareth witness:
    Domine, quis habitabit in tabernaculo tuo, etc.
  'And now will Meed be married   all to a cursed wretch,
To one False-Fickle-Tongue   offspring of a fiend.
Flattery through his fair speech   hath this folk enchanted,
And all is Liar's leading   that she is thus wedded.
  'To-morrow will be made   the maiden's bridal,
And there might thou know if thou wilt   which they be all
That belong to that lordship   the less and the more.
Know them there if thou canst   and keep thy tongue still,
Blame them not, but let be   till Loyalty be judge
And have power to punish them   then put forth thy plaint.
  'I commend thee to Christ,' quoth she   'and his clean mother,
And may no conscience cumber thee   for coveting of Meed.'
  Thus left me that lady   there lying asleep.
And how Meed was married   meseemed in a dream
That all the rich retinue   that with Falsehood reign
Were bidden to the bridal   on both the two sides
Of all manner of men   the mean and the rich.
To marry this maiden   was many man assembled,
As of knights and of clerks   and other common people,
Assessors and summoners [1]   sheriffs and their clerks,
Beadles and bailiffs   and brokers of wares,
Couriers and victuallers   advocates of the Arches—
I cannot reckon the rout   that ran about Meed.
  But Simony and Civil Law   and assessors of courts
Were most privy with Meed   of any man, methought.
But Flattery was the first   that fetched her out of bower,
And like a broker brought her   to be with Falsehood joined.
When Simony and Civil Law   saw the will of them both,
They assented, for silver   to say as both would.
Then leapt Liar forth and said   'Lo here! a charter
That Guile with his great oaths   gave them together,'
And prayed Civil Law see   and Simony read it.
Then Simony and Civil Law   stand they forth both
And unfold the enfeoffment   that Falsehood hath made,
And thus being these fellows   to read out full loud:
  '*Sciant praesentes et futuri, etc.*
  'Wit ye and witness ye   that wander on this earth,
                  [1] See page 202.